All the King's Orphans
Study Guide

by Lynette Carpenter

The following Study Guide is designed to correlate with *All the King's Orphans*. The Study Guide is beneficial for either personal use or as a group study.

All the King's Orphans can be purchased on Amazon or through www.lynettecarpenter.com.

Table of Contents

Week 1 - Adopted..4

Week 2 - Jealousy..7

Week 3 - Poverty..11

Week 4 - Fear..16

Week 5 - Narcissism...22

Week 6 - Control..27

Week 7 - Fatherlessness...32

Week 8 - Insecurity..38

Week 9 – False Humility..44

Week 10 - Deception..49

Week 11 - Hopelessness...55

Week 12 - Pride...61

Week 13 - Shame...67

Week 14 – Esther & Jonah..73

Week 15 – Fathers & Mothers, Absalom and Jezebel..............................82

Week 16 – Ultimate Father & Ways of Royalty.......................................91

WEEK 1
Adopted

Read Preface and Chapter 1

"All the King's Orphans" begins with an allegory. An orphaned child is taken in by a King and He calls her His daughter. Though she is now a princess, the young girl refuses to leave the baggage of her past and take part of Kingdom living.

1. How is this like the body of Christ today?

_____

_____

_____

_____

_____

2. Is Princess Tia's emotional condition one that you can relate to? How so?

_____

_____

_____

3. Earthly adoption is a conscious decision made by a mother and father to offer the security of family, home and provision to a child. How does this correlate with a spiritual adoption by God the Father? In the lines below, write what that looks like to you.

_____
_____
_____
_____
_____

HOW CAN WE KNOW GOD WANTS US AS HIS OWN?

- John 1:12
- John 3:16
- Romans 8:15
- Galatians 4:3-7
- Ephesians 1:4-6
- 1 John 3:1
- 1 John 4:1

Moses could have looked at his life with sorrow. After all, he was denied knowing what it would have been like to grow up with his biological family. What must that have been like for him – born a slave, living as royalty? Was it lonely? Was he accepted? Did he fit in?

It's likely that his heritage was used against him – we don't know. Either way, God was able to take this very unique situation and use Moses to fulfill a pivotal role in earth's history.

Often times our past, our heritage, our situations are used against us. Moses' life is an example of how God uses us no matter who we are, where we came from or what we've done.

Consider the life of Moses.

- What might he have gained from being raised as a prince rather than a slave?
- How would this have affected his mindset?
- How much of a role did this play into his calling to lead the Israelites out of bondage?

Ask yourself:

- What is my purpose in life?

- Am I living with a slave mentality? If yes, what steps can I take to start changing that today?

- How can my life experiences – good or bad - be used to lead others out of bondage?

WEEK 2
Spirit of Jealousy

READ CHAPTER 2

Dana is struggling with a spirit of jealousy and comparison. While her story may seem shallow on some levels, it is an unattractive and all too common problem among Believers – one we hate to acknowledge.

Imagine with me – it's Christmas morning and time to hand out the gifts. You are giddy with excitement because you cannot wait to give the kids in your life their carefully selected gifts. Finally, it's time. You place the wrapped gifts in each child's lap and watch as they tear into it with joy. Your heart is bursting with so much love for these precious children. So much so, you find yourself fighting back a tear.

And then... everything changes. After only a moment of delighting in their own gift, you see those little heads turn and suddenly, you recognize the thoughts running through their heads. "What did she get? Is it better than what I got? Can I still be happy with what I have?"

In our entitled society, it's difficult to raise children counter-culturally, but let's stop and consider how much of these characteristics might be hiding away in our own lives.

SIGNS & SYMPTOMS OF A JEALOUS SPIRIT

- Envious
- Spiteful
- Suspicious of others intent
- Cruel
- Judgmental
- Minimizes others/Maximizes self
- Highly Critical
- Gossips/Slanders

WHAT DOES THE BIBLE SAY ABOUT JEALOUSY?

- Psalm 37:1-3
- 1 Corinthians 13:4
- Philippians 2:3
- James 3:14-16

God has a lot to say about jealousy. While the church of today is often found discussing "big sins", this spirit of jealousy has wounded more of God's children than we realize. It's disgusting and time for it to be exposed and removed from our lives.

An Orphan Spirit compares what others have to their own possessions. Once a son and daughter shed their orphan mentality, they are able to give and receive freely. They know their Dad is the King and He has all they'll ever need.

ASK YOURSELF:

- How do I feel when others receive attention, gifts, admiration or a promotion (whether in the church or out)?

- How do I feel when someone I don't care for gets something good?

- How do I feel when someone I don't care for gets something bad?

- Am I guilty of maximizing me and minimizing others?

- In my opinion, is jealousy a problem in the body of Christ?

- If so, how might the Kingdom of God look different if His children stopped being jealous of one another?

- How can I personally promote a spirit of unity, love and trust?

- What can I do to change me?

Every moment you give to focusing on what others have in comparison to what you don't have – that is a moment wasted. A moment you'll never get back. A moment your Abba Father had hoped you would spend delighting in the good things He has for you.

Don't devote one more moment of your life to the spirit of jealousy.

For further study... look at the life of Elizabeth in Luke 1. Consider how she celebrated her own blessings while at the same time promoted Mary – the unmarried woman who carried an even greater Child than Elizabeth's own. She could have responded so differently. Discuss Elizabeth's attitude and how a different reaction could have affected Mary... or the entire community.

WEEK 3
Spirit of Poverty

READ CHAPTER 3

The subject of the spirit of poverty is one that stirs up division, offense and confusion, leaving many with more questions than answers. Two extremes call out to us – the prosperity message...and those against it. Let's consider the possibility of finding a balance somewhere between the two.

The enemy uses the Spirit of Poverty to keep Believers from accessing all that is available to them from their Abba Father. He convinces the Body of Christ that there isn't enough and never will be enough. The fear of lack keeps the Orphan Spirit clinging to everything they can – essentially filling their lives with that which has little value.

Living with a wealth mindset brings Believers to a place of complete trust in their Abba Father – no matter what how many zeroes are in the checkbook.

For example, Abraham was a wealthy man, yet willingly gave up all he had in order to follow God's calling in his life. His decision to follow God cost Abraham his home, his family, his comfort – even his name.

Western Christianity has reached a level of comfort and security that does not require much faith. If Plan A doesn't work out – we can always rely on Plan B. Our self-reliance has taken us from a place of trust in our Father to trusting in ourselves. The lie hidden within this concept is that we *need* to reach a place of being in control of our life situations, but the truth is that in our sub-consciousness, we know how weak and frail we are – we know our limitations... so while we enjoy the idea of being in control, this also takes us to a place of fear, worry and doubt as we consider what will happen when we reach the end of our resources, strength and abilities.

One aspect of the poverty spirit that is clearly visible in our society is in our health and wellness. Exercise and eating right takes discipline. As you read through the signs and symptoms of a poverty spirit, consider how you might be experiencing the poverty mindset in how you care for your body as well as other areas of your life.

SIGNS & SYMPTOMS OF A POVERTY MINDSET:

- Prone to hoarding
- Blames others
- Unwilling to accept responsibility
- Gives up easily
- Unwilling to sacrifice for something better
- Doesn't consider themselves worth having more

What does the Bible say about the Spirit of Poverty?

- Psalm 23:1
- Psalm 118:8
- Matthew 6:9-13
- Matthew 6:19-34
- John 10:10
- Ephesians 3:14-21
- 1 Thessalonians 4:4-5
- 1 Timothy 6:17

The church proclaims to trust in a God who will "abundantly supply all your needs according to His riches in glory", yet many don't live like they know this to be true. Rather than living generously – without fear of lack, the Orphan Spirit lives tight-fisted, always worried about tomorrow's provisions. This very act denies Abba Father the ability to provide in our time of need.

The welfare system is alive and well in the hearts and lives of many of God's children. It's a way of living that has the Orphan Spirit convinced that the goodness of God isn't available to them unless they follow a list of requirements – making them eligible for His grace and love. It tells a person that if you do this or that in the Kingdom, you will get this or that in return.

Go to church, read your Bible, say your prayers and *hopefully* God will be happy with you.

It's a lie from the enemy! A loving father doesn't extend love only when his kids do nice things for him. No! A loving father loves without reservation. He delights in giving good things to His children. God's desire for His children is that they will come to love Him *not for what they can get out of Him*, but rather that they would come to love Him because His character... His sacrifice... His desperate love so wrecks our broken hearts, we can't help but love Him back.

ASK YOURSELF:

- How is the spirit of poverty affecting my life?

- Do I fear not having enough?

- When things go wrong, how likely am I to blame others for my situation?

- Do I believe that God values me?

- Do I value myself enough to not live with a poverty mindset in my:
  - relationships
  - home
  - health
  - finances

(Discuss what a wealth mindset in each of these areas looks like to you.)

- What can I do to change me?

FOR FURTHER STUDY...look at the life of Joseph.

Consider all he faced – rejection, slavery, betrayal, false imprisonment... yet in each situation, he rose above his circumstances. Had he succumbed to self-pity due to the injustices in his life, billions of lives throughout history would have been negatively affected. His choices to consistently turn his "prison" into a "palace" changed the course of history for the entire world.

WEEK 4
Spirit of Fear

Read Chapter 4

Fear is running rampant in our world today. It is a tool of the enemy and he uses it to his advantage every single day. Sadly, even the church has become a catalyst for fear. Our voices proclaim the message of doom and gloom as loud (if not louder) as the media.

In a world desperate for hope, how can we expect the lost to find joy and freedom in a church full of fear-filled saints?

Fears keep sons and daughters of God from embracing the life He offers. It tells us that we are not enough, unloved, alone, forgotten. It builds a case in our minds that convince us that God is holding out on us, loves other more and, ultimately, that He cannot be trusted.

Those very lies started in the beginning of time. Satan's lies to Eve were just that – "did God really say?" His words implied to Eve that God's word should be called into question. He struck a chord in her heart, building up a fear that God wasn't who He said He was and therefore, she would have to be more, know more and do more in order to be happy.

Sound familiar? How many of us find ourselves running ragged throughout life, desperate to keep everything afloat? We fear letting people down...being abandoned by those we love...dying...not having all we want or need...the list goes on and on.

Consumed by the anxieties, sons and daughters end up missing out on a joy-filled life in their quest to either foster or eradicate their fears. Is fear in your life? Let's analyze our lives and then study what a fearless life looks like.

SIGNS & SYMPTOMS OF A FEAR-FILLED LIFE:

- Elevated heart rate

- Clenched jaw

- Headaches

- Feeling depressed

- Impatient

- Easily angered

- Lack of concentration

- Emotional/cries easily

- Moody

- Trouble Sleeping

- Joyless

- Weight Gain

WHAT DOES THE BIBLE SAY ABOUT THE SPIRIT OF FEAR?

- Psalm 94:19
- Psalm 118:6-7
- Proverbs 12:25
- Isaiah 41:10
- Zephaniah 3:17
- Matthew 6:34
- 2 Timothy 1:7

The Bible is jammed full of verses reminding God's children to not live in fear. In fact, the commands to "fear not" or "be not afraid" are the repeated the most often throughout the Scriptures. Apparently, our Abba Daddy knew the bondage that fear brings.

The beauty of this particular bondage is this – we can walk out of it at the very moment we choose to be free.

How?

Freedom comes when we choose to trust our Heavenly Father. When God tells His children to do something – to not do it is disobedience, correct? So, for example, if God asks you to stop gossiping, yet you continue to slander others, are you walking in obedience?

No. That answer is simple.

Then why do we not look at a failure to trust God as disobedience as well?

I get it... I get it... It's a tough pill to swallow. We've come to believe the lie that fear is a way of life. We live in a broken world where bad things happen – how am I supposed to live fearless when I don't know what tomorrow holds?

Friend, I cannot tell you on these pages what your tomorrow will bring, but I can tell you this – if God is asking you to trust Him, then you need to obey. You need to trust. You may not like the journey He takes you through, but this I know... from where you stand, you cannot see the other side – but He can.

If He tells you, His child, to trust Him with your life, and the lives of those you love, then you need to trust. To not trust is disobedience – and disobedience never brings peace or happiness.

To trust Him means to give up control – which sounds scary, but it's actually one of the greatest gifts God offers you. He desires to see you live happy and free to love and live without the chains of fear wrapped around your soul and killing your body.

Ask yourself:

- Am I living a life of fear?

- How is fear affecting my physical body?

- How is fear affecting my relationships with others?

- Am I guilty of trusting in myself more than trusting God?

- How is fear affecting the Body of Christ?

- What can I do to inspire others to trust God?

- What can I do to change me?

FOR FURTHER STUDY…look at the life of Gideon. Consider how fearful he was, yet he chose to obey God anyway. How many times did Gideon ask God for a sign? How many times did God ask him to give up the things/people that gave Gideon confidence in his own abilities? Gideon needed a lot of reassurance, yes, but he chose to trust in spite of the odds stacked against him – and, ultimately, with God's help he won the battle.

WEEK 5
Spirit of Narcissism

Read Chapter 5

Danny's story is all too familiar. This world is full of narcissistic people – and the church hasn't been immune to it.

Relating to a narcissistic person is exceptionally difficult inside the body of Christ because of our core belief and desire to love one another. We teach humility and servanthood – two things the narcissist preys upon.

When people in the world lives with a narcissistic mindset, people are annoyed – but not surprised. When a person in the church manifests the narcissist characteristics, it can result in devastating blows among the flock – often causing members to walk out the doors for good.

A word of caution – it is intensely difficult for a person to recognize and acknowledge if they are in fact, a narcissist. Below is a list, although not exhaustive, from which you can take a moment to reflect on your own life and determine if you carry a Spirit of Narcissism. If you are uncertain, ask a trusted friend to help you analyze your attitudes and motives. Discovering that you carry this spirit is difficult to accept, but finding freedom is worth it all.

SIGNS & SYMPTOMS OF NARCISSISM:

- Reverts every conversation back to self

- Appearance is everything

- Overtly Arrogant

- Desperate need for admiration

- Bad listener

- Struggles with intimacy

- Takes advantage of others

- Exaggerated sense of self-importance

- Chronic envy

What does the Bible say about Narcissism?

- Psalm 36:1-3
- Proverbs 18:12
- 1 Corinthians 13
- Philippians 2:1-5
- 2 Timothy 2:1-7
- Titus 1:15-16
- 1 Peter 5:5-6
- Revelation 3:17

Jesus calls us to humble ourselves and serve. The Orphan Spirit dealing with narcissism clings to his need for status and approval and ultimately loses out on the blessing of living like Christ. The One who humbled Himself, took on the form of a servant so that He could win you back into a relationship with our Father.

Ask yourself:

- Am I willing to serve those who can give nothing in return?

- Am I willing to listen, without having to insert my own thoughts and opinions?

- Do I look at others as a rung in my ladder? Or do I love without an agenda?

- How do I feel when the attention is on someone else?

- Have I been hurt by a narcissist?

- If yes, what has that stolen from me? Have I forgiven the other person?

- Am I in a narcissistic relationship right now? What should I do to change this situation?

- In your opinion, how has narcissism affected the Western Church?

- What can I do to change me?

The Spirit of Narcissism has crushed millions within the Kingdom. While many find healing, there are thousands who never recover. Since narcissists love status, they are often found in places of leadership which can lead to incredible misuse of power within the church.

If you have been hurt by a narcissistic leader in the past, don't let that be reason enough to keep you from finding a body of believers who better represent the mind of Christ. Forgiveness is the key to setting you free from carrying the hurt any longer.

FOR FURTHER STUDY...read the story of Ananias and Sapphira in Acts 5. Their mutual need for affirmation, lead them to give generously to the church. God knew their hearts though – and He knew they were lying about their generosity as well. Their heart posture so grieved Him, that both Ananias and his wife lost their lives. Their story tells believers today the importance of ridding all narcissism from our lives and learning to love others more than self.

WEEK 6
SPIRIT OF CONTROL

Read Chapter 6

Fear is a seed bed for the controlling personality found in the Orphan Spirit. Living in a world of uncertainties causes the Orphan Spirit to latch on to anything that offers security whether big of small – much like what we see in the spirit of poverty.

On the other side of the coin, there are the unsecured components in the Orphan Spirit's life. Things which are deeply loved and desired...but not guaranteed.

Things like...people.

This leads us to a place of considering two separate scenarios – are you a controller? Or, are you being controlled?

As you study this chapter, first analyze your own behavior. Do you have a tendency to control and manipulate your relationships? And for what purpose?

Second, we will discuss the aspects of being in a controlling relationship. While it is easier to point out the controlling tendencies of others, let's first look at our own lives. To begin, let's look at the signs and symptoms of the spirit of control. As painful as it is, take the time to honestly evaluate your friendships, marriage and other relationships. Ask God to show you the areas of your life where you are letting fear drive you in an attempt to control others.

Signs & Symptoms of the Spirit of Control

- Isolates their victim
- Highly critical
- Makes veiled threats
- Love and acceptance is conditional
- Keeps score
- Uses guilt to manipulate
- Overly jealous
- Micromanages others
- Belittles others
- Argues until they "win".
- Portrays disappointment in others – making them feel as though they don't measure up

What does the Bible say about controlling behavior?

- 1 Samuel 15:22-23
- Matthew 5:3-10
- Matthew 23
- Romans 16:17-18
- 1 Corinthians 13:5
- James 1:26

Matthew 23 is a lot to read, but it brings us to the subject of the controlling nature that can be found in both religion and denominationalism.

While many good things come from the two entities, there is a danger that is often overlooked. This is the aspect of "guilting" people into performance based behaviors. "If you do this, you will be loved and accepted. If you do that, we will condemn you."

The desperate need to belong causes people to conduct themselves in the acceptable manner their denomination or religion requires having little, if anything, to do with what the Father wants for them as an individual.

For example, a young man was part of a conservative denomination. There were many rules for both conduct and dress. One of the rules had to do with a man's facial hair and my friend had broken the rule by growing longer sideburns. The pastor of the church came to him, requiring that he remove the offensive hair from his face – or risk losing his standing in the church.

My friend was upset, but finally agreed. His final words to his pastor were this, "I'll remove the sideburns from my face, but I'll still be wearing them on my heart."

My friend eventually left that particular denomination and ultimately, the church altogether. To this day he sees God as a ploy used to control others and has no desire to pursue a relationship with a God he no longer believes even exists.

As Christians, we need to seek the heart of the Father in how we treat those who do not carry the same convictions as us. Otherwise, we risk pushing forward with what makes us feel good and holy and comfortable while totally missing what God is calling us to.

Ask yourself:

- Am I convinced I cannot be happy unless *other* people make certain changes?

- How do I feel when my spouse or my children make me "look bad"? What is my response?

- If a project isn't going my way, do I tend to micromanage everyone?

- How do I treat those who do not hold the same values as I?

- Do I allow my spouse the freedom to enjoy outside relationships (friends, relatives, etc)?

- If someone I love lets me down, do I remind them often of their failures?

- Do I keep score in my relationships?

- How can I change me?

FOR FURTHER STUDY...look at the life of King Saul.

You'll find much of his story in 1 Samuel. When the nation fell in love with David, King Saul became jealous. He used all his resources to try to control David's life. He chose a wife, a job and a home for David. He could only abide David as long as he, Saul, was in control of David's life. When that control began to slip from Saul's hands, he took the ultimate control in his hands as he attempted time and time again to to kill David.

WEEK 7
SPIRIT OF FATHERLESSNESS

Read Chapter 7

Fatherlessness is the root issue of the problems in our world today. Billions of people fighting their way through life with an overriding sense of emptiness in their soul.

The emptiness only a father can fill.

The emptiness only a *Father* can fill.

Both are needed.

God the Father designed "family" with a specific structure – one that would represent His heart towards His children. Satan desperately hates all that is of God and has made it his goal to destroy one of God's best gifts to humanity – fathers.

Look at our society today – men are no longer men. Somehow we have reached a place where it is ok to openly mock and degrade men. They are portrayed as lazy, dumb, sloppy, valueless humans. Our children are growing up watching this played out in commercials, sitcoms, and society in general.

Men, excuse me for a moment as I have a word to share with my sisters.

Ladies, we need to have a heart to heart. Just you and me.

You need to know something - Satan has a target on your husband's back. He is doing all he can to break down his role in the family through disrespect and mockery – and he's inviting every man's wife to join him in his assault.

I urge you - DO NOT SIDE WITH THE ENEMY!

Your husband is a gift from God and though he may not be the answer to your prayers today, but what would happen if you start being the answer to his?

Think about it - it must be intensely difficult to rise up and be the father and husband he is called to be when the devil is beating him down constantly – but imagine how much more difficult it must be when his own wife has taken up forces with the enemy?

Am I saying that men are victims and without excuse? Absolutely not. Please hear my heart in what I am trying to explain.

Every relationship is different and I acknowledge that. If you are in an abusive or dangerous relationship, you need to seek help… this is not what I'm talking about. What I am saying here is for the woman who has lost respect for her husband for various reasons and has fallen into a pattern of tearing him down.

I beg of you to consider what you are doing!

Disrespectful words will beat the very life out of the best gift God has for us and our children and so often, we don't even realize it. You may think your words hurt only him, but, the truth is, when attacking your partner, you're also hurting yourself in the process.

If you want your husband to rise up and be the man you always dreamed of, you have the power to begin building him up simply by becoming counter-cultural.

You praise him.

You thank him.

You lift him up publicly and privately...and you pray for that man!

You need to begin looking at him as your best gift ever and fiercely protect him.

Too difficult? You have an Abba Father who is capable of healing the hurt in your heart. Ask Him to mend the broken places and give you the strength to love your husband. Too often we as women look to our husbands for fulfillment, value and identity. As wonderful as our husband may be, they are mortals and will eventually fail us – and we them. If we want our marriage to succeed, we must remove this burden from our spouse and find our identity in Christ alone.

He is the *only* source of perfect love and fulfillment.

In the process, you will be saving not only your marriage, but also your children from facing a life of fatherlessness. This, my sisters, will affect not only you, but generations to come. The choice is yours.

Signs & Symptoms of Fatherlessness

- Feelings of abandonment

- Struggles with loneliness

- Low self-worth

- Feels empty inside

- Develops addictions to fill the void or numb the pain

- Clingy in relationships

- Fears being alone or rejected

- Puts up walls

- Defensive and guarded

- Either highly dependent (smothering) or exceptionally independent (detached)

- Feels lost

What does the Bible say about Fatherlessness?

- Deuteronomy 6:6-9
- Psalm 27:10
- Psalm 54:4
- Psalm 68:5-6
- Psalm 103:13
- Psalm 127:3-5
- Proverbs 3:11-12
- Proverbs 22:6
- Isaiah 49:15-16
- John 16:27
- 2 Corinthians 3:2-3
- 2 Corinthians 6:18
- Ephesians 6:4
- 1 Peter 5:7

Fatherlessness affects both men and women...and in so many aspects of life. We see fatherlessness not only in the home, but also in the church. Many people have left the Kingdom over the treatment to or from leadership in the church.

If you are dealing with the pain of fatherlessness, consider where it began and ask God to heal the brokenness. The truth of the matter is this – we are human. We fail. There is not one of us who is perfect and if you are bitter, angry, addicted, lonely or desperate because of a daddy issue in your life, I beg of you to lay your hurt at the feet of the only perfect Father.

He alone can fill that fatherless void in your soul. Once you allow yourself this perfect gift of a Father, every other relationship in your life can be ones without the demands and expectations that have the ability to crush your soul.

Why?

Because in Him, you are complete and able to love without fear. In Him, you will discover that even if *everything* falls apart – He is always, *always* more than enough.

Ask yourself:

- Do I relate to the fatherless aspects of the Orphan Spirit?

- If yes, what situation has caused this?

- Who or what do I turn to for comfort?

- Is this a healthy choice?

- If not, how should I change this?

- Do I carry bitterness towards a father role in my life?

- Do I recognize God as my Father?

- If not, ask God to reveal Himself as a Father to you.

- If yes, what kind of Father do I see Him as?

Your Father God loves you so passionately. If you feel as though you have been abandoned or unloved, don't let another moment go by without reaching your arms up to the Father. He has loved you from the beginning of time and He wants nothing more than to hold you and call you His own.

FOR FURTHER STUDY...read the story of the Prodigal Son in Luke 15:11-32. Focus on the actions of the father and realize that he is a picture of our own Abba Daddy. He is watching for us ready to run and meet us when we turn to find Him.

WEEK 8
SPIRIT OF INSECURITY

Read Chapter 8

Insecurity is a major issue in our world today. While social media has brought much good into our world, it has also birthed an overwhelming amount of insecurity as well. Orphan Spirits have never learned to look to their Father for validation. The idea seems empty, silly and worthless. Thousands, maybe even millions, of Orphan Spirits wearing the garment of insecurity fill the pews each Sunday... their works begging for acknowledgement... their pious lives shrouded in false humility.

It's a common discussion among many – the temptation to compare your life with the lives you see splashed across Facebook, Instagram and Pinterest. Our teens are growing up in a world where the perfectly posed selfie is their source of validation and self-worth, while at the same time suicide rates are rising due to the bullying taking place via the internet.

I personally use social media and am not attacking the use of it itself, I am simply cautioning us in how we rely on it for self0-worth.

We live in a world of people yearning to know they are enough. Desperate to know they are loved. The weak claw frantically at anyone who will tell them the right words while the strong grow a little more cynical with each smothering relationship they encounter.

Insecurity is incredibly prevalent and highly toxic. Most Believers are unaware of how deadly the spirit of insecurity has become - and it *must* be addressed!

I admit that it sounds harsh – but the results of insecurity have so deeply wounded millions inside the body of Christ. We must educate ourselves and be willing to take a deep look into our own lives. This is not a time to be picking others apart. It is a time to do some self-examination and remove the spirit of insecurity in our own lives.

Insecurity is idolatry – it is the worship of self. Few recognize it as such. For so many, acknowledging they are an insecure individual is to offer an excuse for bad behavior. I invite you to look at this deadly spirit and recognize for yourself the danger that comes from living a life full of insecurity.

Signs & Symptoms of Insecurity

- Unable to accept criticism – very defensive

- Is a bully

- Belittles others

- Loves to talk about themselves

- Is a control freak

- Authoritarian

- Compulsive

- Unable to give or receive a compliment

- Insatiable appetite for validation

- Identity is rooted in the Christian lifestyle – rather than in Christ

- Is a people pleaser

- Competitive

- Celebrates other's failures

- Pours on the guilt

- Materialistic

- Presents both arrogance and/or false humility

What does the Bible say about Insecurity?

- 1 Samuel 16:7
- Isaiah 26:3
- Zechariah 4:6
- Matthew 6:31-34
- Romans 12:2-3
- Ephesians 6:10-14
- Philippians 4:6-9
- 1 Timothy 6:17
- 1 John 2:15

There is so much freedom found inside the pages of God's word when it comes to our insecurities.

To live without insecurity means to live at peace with who you are because of who your Father is. It is not with an air of entitlement or pride. No, it is with an attitude of peace, humility and kindness. Sons and daughters who have removed insecurity from their lives are willing to lift others up and serve with a heart of love and compassion. They do not rely on brothers and sisters to fill their love tank and they recognize that the only perfect source of validation comes from their Abba Father.

Ask yourself:

- Do I rely on the compliments of others to make me happy?

- When someone compliments me, do I refute their words? If so, why?

- When someone fails in the church, do I feel compassion? Or do I secretly find pleasure in their situation?

- When someone speaks correction in my life, do I willingly listen? How *do* I feel about that person afterwards? How *should* I feel about that person afterwards?

- Am I busy serving in the church? How busy? What is my motive? If no one noticed, would I still do it?

- When I post on social media, what is my motivation?

- When I'm with others, do I talk about me? Am I good at listening?

- I've been hurt by someone else with the spirit of insecurity – what should I do?

- How can I remove insecurity from my own life? How can I help someone else remove it from theirs?

FOR FURTHER STUDY...

read Isaiah 53 and consider the life of Jesus. The Bible tells us that He had no beauty or majesty to attract us to Him…He was despised…rejected. Meditate on how Jesus was treated by both the "saints" and the "sinners". Yet He chose to die for humanity in spite of the personal attacks, abuse and rejection.

WEEK 9
SPIRIT OF FALSE HUMILITY

Read Chapter 9

False humility in the lives of God's sons and daughters has turned the stomachs of much of society. We can all think of a time when someone in the church tried to appear ultra holy, while trying to sweep a plethora of sin under the rug of their heart...but what about the subtle ways in which we like to present ourselves as better than those around us?

False humility is often difficult to identify – especially if the Orphan Spirit has cultivated a life-long pattern of walking in it. Like the Spirit of Insecurity, False Humility is difficult for the Orphan Spirit to identify in himself.

Many believers have fine-tuned their ability to look the part in the public eye, while living as they wish when no one is watching. People living with false humility within the walls of the church tend to do all they can to look good, but have no love. You will see this in the ones who refuse to serve the least among us – the children and the elderly.

This may sound harsh, but in all reality, the Orphan Spirit looks at others as a means to an end – a rung in their ladder. For example, since children generally cannot offer status to adults, the Orphan Spirit is seldom found *willingly* serving the younger generation of their church and community – although the public approval of leadership might be worth the "sacrifice". The goal of sons and daughters should be to take an *honest* evaluation of their *own* life and consider what their true motives for what they do (or don't do) within the body of Christ.

As you study this chapter, ask God to reveal if you are carrying the spirit of False Humility – and choose to be set free.

SIGNS & SYMPTOMS OF FALSE HUMILITY:

- Advertises personal sacrifices

- Is easily offended

- Believes some jobs are "beneath" them

- Admits small sins but overlooks large ones in their own life

- Quick to judge others

- Fluent in "Christianese"

- Serves others as long as it benefits self

- General apathy towards children or elderly

- Justifies personal sin

- Refuses to change behavior even after an apology

- Use meek body language and humble tone while bragging

- Unable to laugh at self

What does the Bible say about False Humility?

- Matthew 23
- I Corinthians 13
- Philippians 2:3
- Colossians 2:20-23
- James 3:9-12
- James 4:7-12
- 1 Peter 5:5

Once adopted, sons and daughters live transparent lives – often using their past to encourage others to living a life of freedom inside the Kingdom. The Orphan Spirit is tempted to hide where they've been, but can also use their testimony (good or bad) in an effort to lift up self.

Sons and daughters know why they are free and want nothing more than to see their Abba lifted up and glorified. They remember what He's saved them from, and they know that every good thing in their lives comes from Him.

ASK YOURSELF:

- What is my motivation for doing good works?

- How much time do I spend thinking about my position among my brothers and sisters in the church?

- Am I willing to do a job that largely goes unnoticed?

- Am I willing to clean the toilets?

- Can I admit my failures and humbly ask for help to make needed changes in my life?

- Do I love those who can "do nothing for me"?

- How important is it to me to get approval from others – especially church leadership?

- How often do I acknowledge the good of others in the church?

FOR FURTHER STUDY...research the actions and attitudes of the Pharisees in Jesus' day. Their position among the Jewish community demanded respect and awe. They placed religious demands on others that they themselves did not keep and used guilt and manipulation to control their followers.

WEEK 10
SPIRIT OF DECEPTION

Read Chapter 10

The lying tongue is an often used tool of the Orphan Spirit. When you stop to think about it – it only makes sense.

When a child is left out on their own, they use whatever means they have in order to live. This leaves them feeling as though they have no options other than to say what is necessary in order to survive.

After adoption, the Orphan Spirit must renew their mind and recognize that deception is not the answer. Outside the Kingdom walls, lying was a way of life – inside the Kingdom, we discover that truth leads to a life of peace.

Our society is filled with lies. Everyday we must filter through every word we hear and see and determine what is true and what is not. Lies have become such a way of life that for some, it's difficult to speak the truth – even when it doesn't matter.

In this chapter, we are going to look deeper at the spirit of deception and ask ourselves if we are wrapped up in a world of lives.

For some, it will be "small" lies – for others, the lies have grown so astronomical you may question how to unravel yourself from the mess. Wherever you find yourself, when it comes to the spirit of deception, take hold of the knowledge that Satan is known as the father of lies and wants nothing more than to get you to act, live and think like him. If he can do that, he then has access into your life where he will carry out his plan to steal, kill and destroy every good thing God, your Father, has given you.

After all, this father of lies deceived mankind with his lies from the very beginning. His tactics have not changed and he wants nothing more than to convince the children of God to join him in his deceit.

Signs & Symptoms of a Deceiving Spirit:

- Secretive

- Nervousness

- Stays "busy" in order to avoid confrontation

- Uncomfortable praying in public

- Spends little to no time alone with God

- Prayers are "me-centered"

- Preys on the weak

- Builds a case against brothers and sisters

- Causes division

- Will change churches often

- Often involved in drama or chaos

- Feels distant from God

What does the Bible say about a Deceiving Spirit?

- Psalm 101:7
- Proverbs 24:28
- Luke 8:17
- John 8:42-47
- Romans 12:17-21
- Ephesians 4:25
- James 1:26
- James 3:13-16
- 1 John 2:3-6

God makes no secret of how much He despises lying. Lying is what brought sin into this world in the first place – no wonder it so grieves the heart of our Abba.

Many sons and daughters have been wounded by the lies of others - and it's a difficult thing to recover from. If you have been lied about or betrayed by someone you love, recognize it as an attack from the enemy. You can allow the pain of it to keep you from your inheritance, or you can choose to call it what it is (an attack) and claim God's truth over your life.

Deception will always affect our lives here on planet Earth, but we have the power through Jesus to rise above it. Truth is something that should always be pursued in our lives. Consider how many relationships have been destroyed due to deception.

As the family of God, we must never allow Satan to build a case against a brother or sister in our minds. Busyness is a part of the American lifestyle – but with it comes a lack of communication, distance and disconnection. Through that, the Spirit of Deception can wreak havoc in our minds and in our relationships.

My challenge to you is to pursue unity and connection. Don't believe the lies that you are unloved and unwanted. Reach out to those you feel distant from and speak life and blessings over them. It takes humility but it is so worth breaking down those walls of distance and pain – especially when they are built up over false assumptions.

Ask yourself:

- What relationships have I lost due to deception?

- Who have I built a case against in my mind? Are these thoughts truth or simply my perception?

- Do I "fudge" the truth?

- How much time do I spend alone with God?

- Do I portray myself to be something or someone I am not?

- How is my prayer life?

- Are there any areas of my life where I am living a lie?

- If I could peel back all the layers of who I appear to be on the outside, who am I deep inside?

- What has God been speaking to me?

FOR FURTHER STUDY... look at the life of Joseph. Note how often he was lied about, abandoned and used, yet he refused to allow bitterness change him. No matter where he was in life – in the palace or in the prison, Joseph rose to a place of leadership because of his integrity.

WEEK 11
SPIRIT OF HOPELESSNESS

Read Chapter 11

Christians can often be the loudest promoters of hopelessness. Stop and consider how often you pass a church and is yard sign is either negative or condemning. Or both.

In a world of brokenness and despair, Believers have somehow decided that the best way to win the lost is to pile more condemnation, worries and fear to the already overwhelming burdens so many carry.

Satan stands at the gates of the Kingdom proclaiming his messages of fear and doubt – and we, the sons and daughters, are listening. Not only listening, but relaying his message - and pulling more and more of the church into our shared slavery to fear and despair.

The Orphan Spirit has little to look forward to. His future is bleak and offers more of the same – or worse. Though a child of the King, the Orphan Spirit lives a powerless Christian life on this earth. His only hope is that Jesus will come back soon to rescue His children from the brokenness of the world.

But Jesus' death wasn't simply to offer us a free ticket to Heaven. No! His death was a victory over Satan, himself! The truth of the matter is that Satan has *already* been defeated and we are fighting *from* victory! We have the upper hand because of the Cross!

Since we, God's children, are human beings—

made of flesh and blood

He became flesh and blood too by being born in human form;

for only as a human being could He die

and in dying break the power of the devil

who had the power of death.

Only in that way could He deliver those who through fear of death

have been living all their lives as slaves to constant dread.

Hebrews 2:14 & 15 TLB

I believe that God the Father is inviting His children to stop looking out the Kingdom walls at all that Satan is doing and instead, turn our eyes towards Him – our Abba Father.

Have we taken the time to learn who He is?

Have we stopped to consider what He is doing?

Have we asked what life He intends for us to live?

Get to know your Abba – He is your hope!

SIGNS & SYMPTOMS OF THE SPIRIT OF HOPELESSNESS:

- Loss of interest in daily activities

- No passion

- Lack of energy

- Trouble concentrating

- Difficulty sleeping

- Irritable

- Unexplained physical aches and pain

- Suicidal thoughts

- Overall feeling of depression

- Lack of vision or future plans

What does the Bible say about Hopelessness?

- Numbers 23:19
- Job 13:15
- Psalm 3:2-6
- Psalm 16:11
- Psalm 34:9
- Psalm 43:5
- Jeremiah 29:11-13
- John 10:10
- 2 Corinthians 4:16-18
- Colossians 3:1-3

If there's one thing the Devil wants to do, it is to steal the life God intended for His children. John 10:10 tells us this very truth.

You don't have to look very far to find things to steal your joy. Satan jumps on every opportunity to build upon those anxieties. He does this by adding his own spin on what your future might hold. His lies pile high in our minds, tormenting you, robbing you of peace and binding you into a prison of fear.

In this condition, it isn't long before the Orphan Spirit sees nothing worth living for.

Sons and Daughters learn the importance of identifying the lies and rebuking the enemy. We live in a time where bad news is so easily accessible. We have access to countless media sources and have the ability to feed our thoughts without reservation. It is imperative that we choose wisely what we will allow inside the gates of our mind. *Always be on guard, knowing that Satan has a target on your head and knows that if he can gain control of your thoughts, he then has access to your heart.*

Put on the full armor, be alert and prepare yourself for his attacks.

Ask yourself:

- What are my greatest fears?

- Do my fears disrupt my daily life?

- Do I have dreams and goals for my future?

- What dreams have I given up because of hopelessness or fear?

- Were those dreams a calling God put in my heart?

- Do I believe that God is capable?

- Can God be trusted with my life?

- What areas do I need to trust Him more?

- What am I missing out on because of the lies Satan is telling me?
- What are the lies I have been believing?

- How can I be a catalyst of hope in my own church?

FOR FURTHER STUDY...read Numbers 14. Consider how fear kept the children of Israel living in a wilderness for an entire generation. They had a choice – trust in the One who had delivered them from slavery, parted the Red Sea and provided all their needs up to this point – or rely on their own abilities. They chose to act on how they felt and it cost them.

WEEK 12
SPIRIT OF PRIDE

Read Chapter 12

Like the other manifestations of the Orphan Spirit, the Spirit of Pride is self-focus.

The Orphan Spirit has lived a life of self-reliance. At one point in her life, survival and success rested solely on her abilities to make things happen. This mindset brings the Orphan Spirit to a place of looking at people and things as opportunities for advancement.

How can I use you to get what I want?

If others offer no value to the Orphan Spirit, they are cast aside, ignored or abused.

The spirit of pride demands perfection and being number one. It leaves the Orphan Spirit dissatisfied with her marriage, her career success, her physical appearance, her friendships, her finances, her status – even her children. Every area of her life is viewed through the critical lens of pride – and it is crucial that all things measure up to meet her standards.

Pride is incredibly sneaky in that it can mask itself in humility – deceiving the very one carrying the spirit of pride. For example, pride is what causes us to look at our failures and our sins and determine we have no redeeming quality – that our sin is too great for God to forgive.

Stop and consider the arrogance of that belief.

How inappropriate for us to determine the measure of power that lies within the blood of Jesus.

How offensive that must be to our Abba Father.

When so great a sacrifice was made by His Own Son – how audacious of us - frail humanity... how conceited of us to compare *our sin* to *His redemption*... and then *tell Him that He came up short.*

Brothers and Sisters – this is not humility – it is pride.

And it is wrong.

Pride is a devastating disease in our modern church age. Our culture is fueled by self-gain and it's spilled over into the church. It's a sad mentality when we begin to look at our brothers and sisters as a rung in our ladder and we must stop it.

How many of us have been hurt by another in their attempt for self-promotion? And how many have we hurt for the same reason?

Brothers and sisters, it is time lay down our insatiable appetite for man's approval and discover the unfailing love of a Father. His approval is the only one that truly matters and it is time to stop believing the lie that we need to be number one in every area of our lives.

The greatest example is Jesus – Who being in the form of God, did not think equality with God was something to cling to. Instead, He gave up His diving privileges and took upon Him the form of a servant. Not only that, but He laid down His body – bloody and naked – wounded and exposed – all in an effort to pay the price for your adoption into His family.

Knowing that...does having the nicest car, the prettiest hair, the biggest house, greatest talent or the most popular kids really matter?

Think about it.

Signs & Symptoms of the Spirit of Pride:

- Finds fault

- Superficial

- Hungry for attention

- Unwilling to serve the least

- Focused on appearance

- Sees others as objects to be used

- Addicted to comparison

- Lack of compassion

- Lack of discipline

- Sees no need for boundaries

- Refuse to empower others

What does the Bible say about pride?

- Psalm 101:5
- Proverbs 13:10
- Proverbs 16:5
- Proverbs 26:12
- Isaiah 47:10
- Luke 1:49-55
- Galatians 6:3

God's Word is filled with how God feels about pride – and He hates it.

After all, it was the very sin of pride that first got Lucifer cast out of Heaven. When we allow pride in our lives, we open ourselves up to the very same thought patterns that eventually separated Satan from God.

Pride continues to separate. It separates us not only from God but from one another inside the Kingdom. We allow pride to construct walls between us and those "beneath" us while at the same time holding those who intimidate us at arms length.

Sons and daughters must make it a priority to remove pride from our lives and ask our Father to give us the mind of Christ. It is only in this upside Kingdom where the last get to be first, the poor inherit the Kingdom and the greatest is a servant of everyone.

Ask yourself:

- Does it bother me if my friends have something nicer than me?

- A close friend just got a promotion, how difficult is it for me to congratulate them?

- Do I expect others to admire my new car, house, shoes, etc… yet refuse to acknowledge the good things that come into their lives?

- I have the opportunity to promote a friend, do I take it? How does it make me feel?

- Am I accountable to anyone?

- Is my reputation my idol?

FOR FURTHER STUDY... read the life of King Saul. From our first introduction to him, we see a man dealing with insecurities (hiding among the baggage) and later full-blown pride. For example, he was willing to allow a boy (David) attempt to do that which he, Saul, was unwilling to do (kill Goliath). Surely he had to have assumed it was a death sentence for the child, but Saul didn't try to stop David.

At the end of Saul's life, his love of self took him to the lowest point yet – the use of witchcraft. His choices caused his kingdom to be given to his enemy (David) ultimately affecting his children and their children's children.

WEEK 13
SPIRIT OF SHAME

Read Chapter 13

The story of Gomer is a perfect illustration of how shame keeps spiritual sons and daughters from accepting God's forgiveness and living the life God had in mind when He brought us into His Kingdom.

You can read her story in the book of Hosea. Her reputation was not a good one. As a prostitute, Gomer definitely not the ideal prophet's wife. How did she fit into the community? Was she welcomed among the other women of her town? Did the men look upon her with dignity and respect? Was she able to let the past be the past and live in freedom?

Shame is a difficult thing to walk out of – *much more so when brothers and sisters push you down each time you begin to rise up.* The Bible doesn't tell us what Gomer experienced within her community. Perhaps they were welcoming and forgiving.

Perhaps.

I hope they were, but we have all seen or experienced the unforgiving, condemning and judgmental side of Christian society. If that is how Gomer was treated, then how much harder it must have been for her to be able to accept Hosea's love and devotion.

Either way, Gomer's choices were her own to make. Difficult as her life may have been, she can blame no one for the choices she made when she willingly walked away from her husband and children to go back into a life of adultery.

Let's look deeper at the issue of shame and discover how it might be robbing us from the life God has for us.

Signs & Symptoms of the Spirit of Shame:

- No eye contact

- Self-loathing

- Tolerates abuse

- Fatigue (working hard for validation)

- Prone to panic attacks

- Hypersensitive to rejection

- Conducts self-sabotaging behavior

- Struggles with intimacy

- Isolates self

- Creates positions to make themselves indispensable

What does the Bible say about the Spirit of Shame?

- Psalm 34:4-5
- Psalm 103
- Isaiah 43:25
- Zephaniah 3:16-20
- Matthew 11:28-30
- Romans 5:1-8
- Romans 10:11
- 2 Corinthians 4:1-6
- 2 Corinthians 5:17-21
- 1 John 1:9
- ! John 2:28

One of the interesting aspects of shame is its ability to convince a person to self-sabotage many areas of their life. This is a major issue inside the Kingdom. The memory of where we came from provides the perfect material for the Devil to build a case against God's children.

You aren't good enough.

You don't deserve this.

You aren't really loved.

Don't get used to this love - it won't last forever.

His words make sense in the minds of the Orphan Spirit and shame makes itself at home in our heart. Think about it – how has shame affected your life? It may cause you to avoid certain people out of fear that they'll see the real you – and find "you come up short". It may cause you to cut yourself – because "you deserve it". It may convince you to gain back the weight you lost – because "you aren't worth anything anyway". It might be the reason you are stuck in a cycle of poverty – because "you aren't as loved as the other kids in the Kingdom".

Shame is not of God. Think about it!

God wants His children to live a free and abundant life. When we sin, He allows us to feel guilty, but once we have repented, the blood of Jesus removes the sin from our lives and we are forgiven! To continue burying ourselves under those filthy rags of shame is Satan's plan for you – not God's.

And if the people in your life refuse to allow you freedom from your past, you need to move along. It is important to surround yourself with those who will help you see the truth of how God feels about you rather than side with the father of lies and condemn you.

Ask yourself:

- Analyze your internal dialogue. Is it negative? Or truth? Are you able to see the difference?

- Have you sabotaged a relationship, blessing or a gifting in your life? If yes, ask yourself what root fear caused you to do that?

- How transparent are you?

- Do you fear rejection if you were to be completely vulnerable?

- Do you allow others to abuse you?

- Do you abuse yourself?

- Does shame keep you from allowing yourself the gift of a healthy body? Better finances? Peace?

- Is your service in the body of Christ done out of love for God and others or is it to win the approval of God or man?

FOR FURTHER STUDY... look deeper into the story of Hosea and Gomer. Notice how God used Hosea and Gomer's lives to illustrate His compassion and love for the Israelites. That love and compassion is for us today as well.

Read Hosea 14 and accept your Abba Father's lavish love for you today.

WEEK 14
ORPHAN SPIRIT
JONAH AND ESTHER

Read Chapters 14-15

We've taken an in-depth look at some of the root issues found within the Orphan Spirit. While it is incredibly easy to identify these characteristics in the lives of others, finger pointing is not where personal freedom is discovered. Each of us can only experience the joy of living as a spiritual son or daughter within the Kingdom of God by having a transformation within our own mind.

Romans 12:2 says, "Do not conform any longer to the pattern of the world, but be transformed by the renewing of your mind."

The pattern you once knew was the lifestyle of fatherlessness, but if you have been adopted into the Kingdom, your orphan life is in the past. Now begins the process of transforming your thought patterns from the Orphan Spirit to that of a spiritual son or daughter.

What is truth? Who are you? Do you belong?

The truth is that the price has already been paid for you to take your place in the Kingdom of God as His child. So do you belong? How much more would God have to do to convince you that He wants you? Was the price He paid (His Son's death) not enough?

Take a moment to ask your Abba Daddy to reveal ways that you have not yet abandoned your Orphan mentality.

Write down what He is saying to you in each of these areas:

Jealousy_____

Poverty_____

Fear_____

Narcissism_____

Control _____

Fatherlessness_____

Insecurity_____

False Humility_____

Deception_____

Hopelessness_____

Pride_____

Shame_____

The following is Romans 8:1-17 paraphrased from the Message. Read it aloud, placing your name in the blanks.

LIFE ON GOD'S TERMS

When I, _____, entered into Christ's being-here-for-us, I no longer had to live under a continuous, low-lying black cloud. **A new power is in operation in me,**

_____.

The Spirit of life in Christ, like a strong wind, has magnificently cleared the air, freeing me from a fated lifetime of brutal tyranny at the hands of sin and death.

God went for the jugular when He sent His Own Son. **He didn't deal with the problem as something remote and unimportant.** In His Son, Jesus, He personally took on the human condition, entered the disordered mess of struggling humanity in order to **set it right** once and for all. The law code, weakened as it always was by fractured human nature, could never have done that.

The law always ended up being used as a Band-Aid on sin instead of a **deep healing** of it. And now what the law code asked for - but I, _____, couldn't deliver – this law code is accomplished when I, _____, instead of redoubling my own efforts, simply embrace what the Spirit is doing in me.

When I, _____, think I can do it on my own, I, _____, end up obsessed with measuring my own moral muscle but never gets around to exercising it in real life.

When I, _____, trust God's action in me, I, _____, find that God's Spirit is in me—living and breathing God!

Obsession with self in these matters is a dead end; attention to God leads me out into the open, into a spacious, free life. **Focusing on me is the opposite of focusing on God.**

_____ completely absorbed in _____ ignores God and ends up thinking more about_____ than [about] God and what He is doing - and God isn't pleased at being ignored.

But if **God Himself has taken up residence in my life,** I can hardly be thinking more of myself than of Him. Anyone, of course, who has not welcomed this invisible but clearly present God, the Spirit of Christ, won't know what we're talking about. But for the one who welcomes Him, in whom He dwells—even though I, _____, still experience all the limitations of sin— I, _____, will experience life on God's terms.

It stands to reason, doesn't it, that if the alive-and-present God who raised Jesus from the dead moves into my life, He'll do the same thing in me that He did in Jesus, **bringing me, _____, alive to Himself?**

When God lives and breathes in me (and He does, as surely as He did in Jesus), I, _____, am delivered from that dead life. With His Spirit living in me, my body will be as alive as Christ's!

_____, don't you see that you do not owe this old do-it-yourself life one red cent? There's nothing in it for you - nothing at all. The best thing to do is give it a decent burial and get on with your new life. God's Spirit beckons. **There are things to do and places to go!**

This resurrection life I, _____, received from God is not a timid, grave-tending life. It's adventurously expectant, greeting God with a childlike *"What's next, Papa?"* God's Spirit touches my spirit and confirms who I really am.

I, _____, know who He is, and He knows who I, _____, am: **Father and child**. And I know I'm going to get what's coming to me —an unbelievable inheritance!

I, _____, go through exactly what Christ went through. If I go through the hard times with Him, then I'm certainly going to go through the good times with Him too.

~*~

Isn't that beautiful? God went for the jugular when He set things right for you and for me. In spite of that reality, life gets in the way and we tend to forget that beautiful truth. When difficulties come our way, we have the choice to respond as sons and daughters – or we can respond with the insecurities and self-focus of an Orphan Spirit.

Jonah and Esther were two Old Testament characters who were called to do great things. Both dealt with fear. Both spent time in prayer and both saw God's hand move miraculously – yet their attitudes were vastly different.

ON THE FOLLOWING PAGE, USING THE LIVES OF JONAH AND ESTHER write out several differences you see in which they approached their calling.

Jonah

Esther

What is a difficult situation you are currently facing in life?

Write out how you could respond as an Orphan Spirit and then how you could respond as a son or daughter. Take a moment to reflect on what results each have the potential to bring into your life

Orphan Spirit

_____

_____

_____

_____

_____

_____

_____

_____

_____

_____

Sons and Daughters

WEEK 15
Spiritual Fathers & Mothers

Spirits of Absalom and Jezebel

Read Chapters 16-17

Our pastors, elders and other church leaders are our spiritual fathers and mothers – yet they are not immune to the Orphan Spirit. The Orphan Spirit is one who desires status and notoriety, and for that reason our church leaders are ones who struggle to lead and serve for the proper reasons.

Pastors need to recognize that part of their calling is to lead the people in their churches, yet at the same time they are there to serve. Unfortunately, many have taken on the role of pastor in an effort to feed their ego. This is completely contradictory to the calling of a pastor. If a church leader looks at his flock as a people who can be used, manipulated and controlled for his own benefit, he has sorely misunderstood his function.

Men and women who have been called to lead the body of Christ must recognize the importance of leading like Jesus. He is the ultimate example in servant leadership.

Imagine a church with leaders who call out the potential in their congregation. Who recognize talents and abilities and provide opportunities to use that gifting. Pastors and leaders must always be aware of the tendency within the Orphan Spirit to compare, control and minimize others. This can make or break a ministry.

How?

Consider the congregation whose pastor refuses to share the load of ministry with his or her flock. The deep-seated need to control has the pastor micro-managing every aspect of church life. If someone steps up with the ability to do something well, the pastor, Sunday School teacher, worship leader, elder... you fill in the blank, may find himself comparing his own ability to that person. If the Orphan Spirit mentality takes over, the lay member is refused the opportunity to use his gifting – or is sent in a different direction.

"What if I let her teach and she does better than I do? Maybe she should help with hospitality."

"What if he sings better than me – and people notice? I'll ask him to help the usher team."

"He is a dynamic speaker – I better watch him for that Absalom spirit!"

Done over and over again, the pastor (and other leaders) ends up exhausted, discouraged and lonely with a congregation full of frustrated, unfulfilled, disengaged people.

Christ's example on earth teaches us as leaders the importance of laying down our lives for others. As parents, we are called to set aside our own wants and preferences time and again as we raise our children - and we do it out of a love and desire to see them succeed in life. In the same way, pastors and leaders must discover ways to open doors of opportunity for their congregation.

Less of me – more of you.

Our minds cannot even begin to imagine what all could happen in the Kingdom when all sons and daughters begin to celebrate and promote one another.

At the same time, lay members have a responsibility in being willing to be lead. Both sides have an obligation to serve.

If competition must exist, let's create a culture of competition where sons and daughters attempt to out-serve, out-love and out-promote one another. Wouldn't that be fun?

But prepare yourself – love like this tends to draw a crowd.

Ask yourself:

- How independent am I?

- Am I willing to accept guidance in my life?

- How much do I value and respect my Pastor?

- Am I willing to speak or listen to negativity about my church leadership?

- Do I promote division in my church?

- Do I pray for my Pastor?

(For Pastors and Leaders) Ask yourself:

- Do I lead as an Orphan Spirit?

- As a leader, am I motivated by love or by fear?

- What gives me the most joy in the role I carry?

- Am I a servant-leader? Am I willing to serve or are some jobs in the church "beneath" me?

- How am I promoting members of my congregation?

- Do I fear losing my position? How is this affecting my ability to lead?

- Do I control, manipulate or minimize those I lead?

- How can I be a better leader?

The stories of Absalom and Jezebel are intriguing and both the Absalom and Jezebel spirits or mindsets can be found in our modern day churches. Their stories provide insight into how the Enemy uses people within the Kingdom to destroy the Kingdom. Their target is leadership, but they divide and conquer all that they can along the way.

The life of Absalom can be found in 2 Samuel 13-18. His life was one fueled by an injustice he couldn't forgive. This bitterness led him to do things he never could have imagined at one point in his life.

Jezebel's story is found in both 1st and 2nd Kings. She was the wife of King Ahab and was known as a wicked and idolatrous queen. She lived a life caring for no one but herself, willing to kill innocent people in order to get her way.

Nothing good came to either Absalom or Jezebel and both their lives ended in a disgusting manner.

As you read the signs and symptoms of the Absalom and Jezebel spirits, ask God to reveal any areas of your own life where you may be susceptible to these mindsets. At the same time, consider your friendships. Are you friends with an Absalom or

Jezebel Spirit? Those close to both Absalom and Jezebel found themselves constantly dealing with drama, manipulation and control. Siding with an Absalom or Jezebel Spirit comes at a great cost and it is vitally important that we as sons and daughters are always alert, watching for their next move.

Signs & Symptoms of Absalom

- Distrustful

- Veiled bitterness

- Independent

- Has hidden agendas

- Insatiable appetite for authority

- Charming

- Divisive

- Catalyst for rebellion

Signs & Symptoms of Jezebel

- Attacks the weak

- Seeks approval of leadership

- Defensive, pushy and domineering

- Self-seeking, self-promoting, loud

- Religious

- Deceitful

- Often married to a "weak" spouse (an Ahab)

- Pursues positions of authority

- Is vengeful

As we consider the Absalom and Jezebel spirit, we must recognize that both are after leadership positions. Pastors are often targeted by these spirits and many churches have been destroyed because of it.

In our home, we have made it clear that our children are loved and protected. This knowledge creates an innate desire for our children to protect us – just as we protect them. It's a natural reaction. Think about how easy it is to offend someone by cutting down their mama. Or how many "my-dad-is-bigger-than-your-dad" arguments have we chuckled over? This same basic, fundamental protection for our fathers and mothers of our churches should be the culture inside the Kingdom.

It should be common.

Desired.

Expected.

Take it upon yourself to promote a culture of love and support for your church leadership. Pray for them daily and don't back down when you recognize the characteristics of Absalom or Jezebel making their way into your congregation.

On a personal level, ask God to reveal any areas in your life where you carry these spirits. It is only through an awareness, repentance and God's restorative power that one can walk free from these dangerous and divisive spirits.

WEEK 16
ULTIMATE FATHER WAYS OF ROYALTY

Read Chapters 18-19

Our Father God knows us intimately – but He longs for us to know Him as well. Many people have asked how to know when God is speaking to them. This question always brings to mind an illustration we have done with our youth group.

Consider this – suppose you are in a large room of people. Everyone is talking and you are blindfolded. You are told to go find your dad. You listen to the noise and soon you hear your name called. You immediately dismiss it, because you know that wasn't your father. Soon everyone in the room is saying your name, but there's that one voice – that tone you recognize so well... your dad.

For some of us, the sound of his voice brings discomfort due to a painful childhood. For others, hearing your dad call your name evokes love and anticipation. Earthly fathers are often how we envision our Heavenly Father – and that can be helpful, but it isn't always accurate.

Our Abba Father is a good Father. Satan tries to distort our view of Him – from day one he had Eve doubting God's character. If he did that to Eve, we can know and expect that he will do that to us as well.

When a child is adopted, it's important for the parent and child to spend time together to build a bond that cannot be broken. Our adopted Father is always ready to spend time with you and I – it is vitally important for us to take time with Him. He's always with you – be aware of His presence and soon you will recognize His voice – no matter how many other things are calling out for your attention.

Characteristics of Abba Father:

- Loving

- Compassionate

- Trustworthy

- Nurturing

- Perfect

- Protector

- Generous

- Forgiving

What does the Bible say about God as our Father?

- Deuteronomy 1:31
- Psalm 18:30
- Psalm 103:13
- Isaiah 49:13-16
- Isaiah 64:8
- Jeremiah 31:3
- Matthew 7:11
- Galatians 4:6
- James 1:17
- 1 John 3:1

Ask yourself:

- Do I acknowledge that I have been adopted in the Kingdom of God?

- Do I live like I am a child of the King?

- What area do I struggle in the most?

- How do I plan to change me?

The Ways of Royalty:

Below, list the characteristics you would expect to see in the son or daughter of a king. As you write, consider how well you carry those attributes in your own life.

_____   _____

_____   _____

_____   _____

_____   _____

_____   _____

_____   _____

_____   _____

_____   _____

Who am I?

We've studied many aspects of the Orphan Spirit and hopefully we have reached a place where we can acknowledge who we are in Christ.

Adopted. Forgiven. Loved. Free.

Do you belong?

Yes, you do. We all have a unique role within the Kingdom. Knowing this, may we choose to love one another well as we celebrate the new life we now enjoy as sons and daughters of the King.

> Is it not true that in You the orphan finds mercy?
>
> Hosea 14:3

Made in the USA
Lexington, KY
24 May 2016